Living with Depression– and WINNING

In His love,

"Sarah"

Winola Wells Wirt

Psalm 16:10, 11

Living with Depression– and WINNING

Sarah Fraser

TYNDALE HOUSE PUBLISHERS, INC.
Wheaton, Illinois
COVERDALE HOUSE PUBLISHERS LTD.
London, England

Library of Congress Catalog Card Number 74-21972
ISBN 8423-3680-X
Copyright © 1975 by Tyndale House Publishers, Inc.,
Wheaton, Illinois. All rights reserved.
First printing, January 1975
Printed in the United States of America

Thanks be to God, which giveth us the victory.
1 Corinthians 15:57

CONTENTS

FOREWORD

Occasionally we meet an individual who, in modern terms, can "put it all together." Such a person is Sarah Fraser. In her autobiographical tale *Living with Depression—and Winning* she documents as a Christian witness the dreary and often discouraging pathway of emotional illness. Her trail of manic-depressive illness is one that is traveled by many people. It is a trail that often starts with a young adult and is characterized by deep depressions, flights of euphoria, or combined emotional disturbances. Although the sieges of illness are self-limited, the attacks are potentially destructive to an individual's self-confidence.

Sarah vividly depicts these swings of individual emotion. She describes, as no psychiatric textbook has been able to do, the inner doubts and fears of a traveler on the manic-depressive highway. The deep understanding and insight she possesses are expressed in an engrossing, often humorous account of her journey.

Like the Apostle Paul, she documents her travels as a Christian witness, and her journey is a testimony to the God she worships. The book illustrates in a vital way what God and Christ can mean to each one of us personally. Without divine help she might have been defeated. Sarah gives us a heartwarming and human example of faith in this book. For it is faith, and particularly Christian faith, that sustains our daily hope for the New Tomorrow.

"I will all the more gladly boast of my weaknesses, that the power of Christ may rest upon me. For the sake of Christ, then, I am content with weaknesses, insults, hardships, persecutions, and calamities; for when I am weak, then I am strong" (2 Corinthians 12:9, 10, RSV).

Brian Williams, M.D.

1
ISN'T THERE ANYTHING?

The middle-aged woman crouched on a little homemade island in the center of her bed. She rocked back and forth like a toy rollabout, moaning eerily.

"I've lost all her money! I've lost it all! Mother worked so hard to save it, now I've lost it! I wanted her to have it for her old age but I've lost it! I've lost it!"

Her voice grew hoarse with the alternate screaming and moaning. How do I happen to know about this sad scene? I was present. *Dear God, I was that woman!* But it was many months before I was to become aware of the nature of my trauma.

Events began unheralded on a trip to the East Coast to see my mother. On each trip I wondered if I would see her again in this life. She was always gentle and affectionate; her frailty made her seem only a breath from the next world.

Mother's doctor, and mine in years past, gave me a thorough going-over with various tests in the hospital nearby. Summary time came. The doctor, brilliant in my estimation, said as she waved me into a seat, "Sarah, clean bill of health! Except for a minor infection that can be cleared up quickly. But you feel miserable, don't you?"

She had known me a long time. "Yes," I admitted wearily, "I do. Isn't there anything . . ." my voice trailed off.

My doctor sounded more kind than ever. Leaning over her big desk toward me she said, "You know I'm not a psychiatrist . . ."

Oh, no! I thought, wondering what she would say next.

"I can give you medication that may help some, but I really feel you should be in touch with a clinic or some doctor who can provide you with psychiatric care. You don't have to decide right now, but I know you want to be well. Talk it over with your husband. You owe it to him to be as well as you can be."

Of course she was right.

I had been home only a short time when my husband's superior called him in. "What's the matter with your wife?" he asked.

Marcus hesitated. "I don't know. She just had a complete physical."

"I'd like my doctor to look at her. We'll arrange the appointments."

A few days later the pale April dawn thrust a

chill into me; more sinister was the coldness of fear within.

"You shouldn't be doing this, James," I protested to our friend and co-worker. "Marcus could have taken me."

Now he was looking at me so kindly and shaking his head negatively. "Marcus is more than busy; besides, Sarah, I want to take you and introduce you to the doctor. You'll feel confidence in him; we all do."

"I'm more grateful than I can say," I told him. "So is Marc."

Indeed I was to discover that my inner quavers would lessen as we drove to the clinic in the next town. By the time we arrived I was calm, enjoying the first few hours of relief from depression I had known in a very long while.

James arranged for my room in a hotel, then we went to the clinic. As soon as he had introduced me to Dr. Blake, James bestowed a brotherly good-bye kiss and started back.

Dr. Blake was more than kind. We talked for a while; it didn't seem like a consultation with an extremely busy and noted internist.

Tests and X rays galore followed for over a week. I began to feel like one of the cards that were piling up in my permanent file as I was propelled from one department to another.

In each waiting room I found people sitting motionless, wearing expressions of discouragement. They seldom glanced up. During the day I was kept busy with the clinic routine, but when I returned to the hotel at night, I felt bereft. It was Holy Week, and I attended church in town. The evening services solaced me. As the days wore on, my diet became restricted and I was increasingly uncomfortable.

At the beginning of the second week Dr. Blake called me in. I had expected to be finished in three or four days, but things seldom work out so simply for me. The doctor was courtly, as usual. "We feel that in order to rule out certain symptoms, you should have minor surgery."

I was delighted! Anything that was positive, anything that smacked of action to get me out of my slough of despond sounded wonderful.

The surgical procedure was my briefest hospital sojourn, about twenty-four hours. Then I was again summoned to Dr. Blake's office. Three or four men rose as I entered. Dr. Blake introduced us, then motioned me to a seat near his desk.

First the learned doctors told me what I didn't have! Then a tall psychiatrist with piercing brown eyes told me what I did have. He was brief, but not abrupt. I don't recall that he smiled; I could have used one then. I glanced over at that wonderful Christian, Dr. Blake, and he was looking at me with such kindness and commiseration. That was better than a smile, I decided.

Bringing my gaze back to the chief, I wondered whether he was saying it for the first time or repeating it, or was it an echo in my heart that would haunt me for the rest of my life? I don't know, but the words were, "You are a cyclothymic personality and we urge immediate psychiatric care."

I reeled inwardly, then rallied enough to ask, "Can you please make a referral? I have no idea where to go."

The good doctor was ready to oblige. He recommended a certain Dr. Bergman in my town. His dreadful sentence hung in the air. I couldn't pass it off as a nightmare. It was broad daylight, and just then the sun was shining brilliantly. I could hardly believe my own affirmation at the time, but I said to myself the three words that have enabled me to travel this far along a sometimes stony path, "God is able."

My pride hurt as much as my body. *Dear God,* I cried inwardly, *I couldn't be mentally ill, or emotionally disturbed, or however one chose to describe the sickness. Nobody, but nobody, in my family had ever been so afflicted.*

In similar moments of near panic since that day, I have found that if I can become interested in someone, the fears lie down or go away for a while. As we recall the story of our Lord's temptation, we are reminded that even the devil granted surcease for a time (Luke 4:1–13).

5

But there I was, still sitting in Dr. Blake's office. The semicircle of specialists was rising, preparing to depart, obviously waiting for me to do likewise. They left as soon as I stood; I lingered to thank Dr. Blake and to say good-bye. Unconsciously I was hoping for his word of comfort.

2
WORDS ON A PAD

I could not get an immediate appointment with Dr. Bergman. I wished somehow that while I was under the knife they had extended the surgery to the removal of my imagination. That evening I began picturing long lines of people all over the world in need of far more care than there were psychiatrists to administer it. What a sad sight! And dreariest of all was the last person in each of the hundreds of lines—Sarah Fraser.

Such cheerless art forms put me into a mood that was something less than sunny. In fact, I was desperate. My husband belongs to the "do something" school. I tearfully asked him not to call the doctor; I would just have to wait another week until my appointment.

He kept right on thumbing through the phone book. "If you think I'm going to sit by and . . . here he is."

"They hate to be called at home," I wailed.

"I don't always enjoy it either," he said, "but I take the calls. Dr. Bergman?"

Marcus made out a good case for my condition but the ice cubes started falling all about him.

"You don't take any emergency cases? My wife isn't really that, though she is suffering badly from nerves. Yes? The appointment made last week? Thank you, sir, and good night."

"Met your match, honey? Thanks for trying. I've dimmed your evening enough. Think I'll go to bed."

The day of my appointment was bleak and rainy. It seemed appropriate. Briefly into my troubled mind trickled the biblical words, "This is the day which the Lord hath made; we will rejoice and be glad in it" (Psalm 118:24).

Then the negativism that clutched at me continually took over. "This is the day which *I* have made—the day in which I must admit my defeat publicly—the day I go for my first appointment with the psychiatrist. And what good will that do *me*?"

Every move proved an effort of the will as I readied myself for the trip downtown. Alternately shivering and perspiring, I managed a few swallows of coffee and fruit juice, dutifully taking a vitamin pill. The bus to the medical center took an aeon; no, no, it traveled too fast!

I saw the huge building on the corner. Like a

stranger a few feet away, observing for a class paper, I saw myself pushing sagging shoulders against the revolving door as I headed toward the building directory. I had written the suite number on a slip of paper. This was a delaying action; even the elevator was ready to go up. No further postponement was possible. Floors were called out; mine was the last—the nineteenth. I wondered whether the elevator girl knew. Were there any "regular" offices on this floor—for nice pregnant young housewives or people with lovely organic problems? Yes, *lovely*, for where breathes a psychiatric patient who would not gladly swap his intangible fears for physical problems which can be removed or treated.

I remembered my ten days of extensive tests and minor surgery, and how I had been forced to face the bitter truth of mental illness, suspected previously. Symptoms? Very real, but functional, caused by emotional disturbance. Beneath their professional words, I had sensed a certain sympathy as the doctors made their diagnosis: "Cyclothymic personality . . . immediate psychiatric care."

My stomach knotted again as the elevator came to an abrupt stop. Had I thanked the elevator operator, as was my policy toward those in a rather claustrophobic occupation? I didn't know. Studying the numbers on the doors, I saw an open one nearby. *The* one. Once I stepped over that threshold, would I be on the long road back to normality, or did hopelessness await me? Financial problems for sure, I thought wryly.

It was a tiny office, the few furnishings adequate and clean, if worn looking. The lighting was good; the literature surprisingly so, even current. Something for children too. Were there little patients? Or did they come from necessity, accompanying a parent? I wondered, too nervous to read the magazines or the leather-bound cartoon scrapbook.

On the pale gray walls were a couple of prints by a French impressionist. My artistic choices revert to earlier centuries, but perhaps the very vagueness of these were psychologically sound for such a locale.

No stiffly starched guardian with a professional smile greeted me from behind a half partition; only an inked sign to ring Dr. Bergman's bell. Obviously he was busy with a patient. Should I ring the bell now, or wait? Finally I gave it a quick touch; no one came. In about five minutes there were sounds of a door opening and brief good-byes. A taut but nice-looking man, around thirty-five I judged, avoided my eyes and my feet in the cramped quarters and went quickly out the door. I felt a sense of embarrassed kinship.

The doctor turned toward me as I rose hastily. "Mrs. Fraser, you are a little early for your appointment." He turned and went back to the inner sanctum. He had smiled pleasantly enough but had not offered to shake hands. I felt a bit hurt, but that was par for the course these days—though it seemed to me, conversely, that some people had been unusually kind, especially those who *knew*. Rather awkwardly I sat down again. I could smell the cigarette the psychiatrist was finishing. Did he need to try to compose himself before he could leap from the problems of the earlier appointment into an approach to my needs? I was finding it increasingly wearing to wonder what everyone was thinking. By what nightmarish series of events was I here at all?

With a bit of grim amusement I realized that while the psychiatrist might need composure to face me, I was here for my precise lack of it.

Presently he returned, reached for my coat and placed it on a hanger in a small closet, then ushered me into another tiny room. This was square, with two more French prints on the walls and one large window with a panoramic view of the city. There was a glass protector over the lower part of the open window, behind and over which a chill wind was blowing, in contrast to the heat of the outer office.

I rose hastily and walked out to the closet, retrieving my coat, explaining my abrupt act as I reentered the room. If Dr. Bergman had thought I might be about to run away, he gave no indication, merely remarking that it was a cool east wind but making no move to lower the window. I wondered if the climatic arrangement was for the comfort of the patient or the interrogator.

I indicated a picture on his desk. Unless we, or I, could establish a basis of rapport, I simply could not sit there and chip off pieces of my soul to put on a charger like St. John's head. "Who's the pretty lady?" I asked.

He smiled broadly. "My wife."

The person in the photograph looked considerably younger than he, though I began to sense that his hair might be prematurely white, his ruddy complexion and rather heavyset body not an indication of age but natural makeup.

"Very good taste in your selection."

"Thank you."

He did not sit at the desk, but in a chair a few feet away. He indicated a chair for me beside the desk. There was a couch, not too comfortable looking. At current rates I thought perhaps I deserved it, but possibly that was reserved for later interviews.

His gray office coat melted into the walls. He pulled a large lined pad toward him, as if about to write the first draft of a high school essay. Then the interview began—a quiet question here and there, but mostly writing, writing . . . I wondered what was important and what wasn't. I wished I could just play a record; I was so tired of thinking and feeling, yes, and *being* . . . I must be fair; the man couldn't help without knowledge, but could he help even then? The now familiar sensation of panic started to beat its dreadful tattoo: *Say something funny; don't give in*, I thought frantically even as I heard my own voice go smoothly on. Somehow I had to stop that unrelenting pen; was it recording what I should disclose, or had I lost my sense of values?

"I talk rather well, don't I?" I inserted casually, as if that sophisticated remark would assure him of my sanity.

The psychiatrist looked up with a brief, controlled smile. "Yes, but there are so many details on some things . . . a confused picture so far. I haven't been able to sort out any real pattern to the depression yet."

Sadly I agreed, "I know; it doesn't seem to follow the design of any case histories I have been aware of. It seems incredible that I am here at all. I know it's silly to ask you at this point, but do you think you can help me?"

He refused to compromise his professional integrity. "I don't know. You say you are so frightened. Why? About what? Do you feel that your religious faith has somehow failed you?"

I thought carefully. "No, except that it seems that if it were as strong as I had always supposed, I wouldn't be in such a condition now. I presume my fright stems from the fear of mental illness—also that continued functional disorders (caused by emotional strain) will eventually become organic trouble spots unless I learn inner control."

He was not callous, but there was little warmth to his personality. Perhaps one in his field had to develop detachment.

At one point in his rapid writing, I said earnestly but with a smile, "Doctor, I think I ought to warn you that I am very dramatic. I feel now as if I were standing on a street corner observing this, perhaps with a newspaper article in mind. I don't know how much trouble I'm really in and how much has been conjured by my vivid imagination. The suffering seems painfully real to me though. I know that I've always been inclined to exaggerate. Perhaps you should discount my remarks about 50 percent."

His lips curved noncommittally as he looked up briefly, then continued writing.

I felt like beating my breast and crying out, "Look, I'm dear in God's sight. I'm dear to some people. I don't care about being dear to you, but I *am* human. I need a speck of hope so badly right now." Then I wondered, "Is my public personality showing again? Am I trying to be a Personality Kid to this professional listener at 50¢ a minute?" Drawing an imperceptibly shaky breath, I tried to marshall some more helpful facts for his records. But I wondered, Was I a typical middle-aged woman whose frightened predicament was evident in spite of controlled tones and occasional flashes of humor?

Well, if there was ever a place to let the

pathological petticoats show, this was it. The psychiatrist seemed so inscrutable; I didn't know whether I was succeeding in baring my soul or just babbling. Perhaps this man's cool poise was intentional, necessary to his profession.

I felt an urge to let go with a verbal firecracker, let him know I knew a thing or three about psychiatry. "You know," I began, "I've regressed my conscious mind as far back as possible, in an effort to uncover any reasons for my present state, any contributing factors. It's true I was the only child of a widow, and I loved my mother, grandmother, and aunts devotedly, but I was also fond of my grandfather and uncles too. I never had any sex experiences in childhood, or prior to marriage; I was really a 'good girl'; I loved school and always had fine marks. Of course I was far from perfect, but there is no neat little package of abnormality that we could pounce on and say, 'That's it!'"

Dr. Bergman nodded slightly; any tangible reaction seemed to comfort me. Perhaps my husband and close friends had been too gentle, too sympathetic . . . well, if I needed the clinical approach, I was getting it!

There were several telephone interruptions. "I am not here to confess my family's faults and mistakes, but mine. I'm that dreadful combination—a perfectionist and a pack rat."

Down on the pad went my words; they were

on the second or third large sheet, I noticed. I wished he would let me read them before the next interview; I was beginning to wonder what I had told him.

He stood up abruptly. "I'm afraid our time is gone." Leafing through an appointment book, he added, "Could you come in a week from today?" He hesitated, looked back a few pages. "Perhaps later this week would be better. Could you come in on Thursday morning?"

I knew I must leave, but I hovered pitifully in spite of my better judgment. "I know I shouldn't ask you again, but do you suppose you can help me?"

His half smile was definitely frosty as he propelled me toward the door. "I don't know. Good-bye, Mrs. Fraser."

Outside in the wee anteroom was another patient. I had supposed myself the last before the noon hour. Had he heard my last remark to the psychiatrist? Did it matter?

He was a handsome, sensitive-looking young fellow, early twenties probably. Our glances met.

Cold comfort for you, poor boy, if he's as he was with me, I thought. Then I smiled impulsively and said quietly, "I'm going to pray now for you and me, too."

He smiled back a "thank you" and rose to follow the doctor into his cold gray cubicle. The door closed behind their muted greetings.

I sank down on the settee briefly. At least I

would get warm before leaving. Wistfully I thought, "I feel like a tired old tramp dog who has just lifted an ailing paw to a white-haired stranger, my eyes pleading with him, 'My paws aren't just worn out, are they? There *is* an imbedded cinder or *something* you can take away and help me back to normal?'"

Rising wearily to my feet, I thought, "No snap answers for the dog either."

As I waited for the elevator, I pondered the difference in sensitivity between dogs and humans. Surely I was living in these days in a state of suffering based on feelings more than on facts. Though there were plenty of alibis for my condition, I knew they would no longer serve me wisely or well.

Could I be retrained to face reality? How many times would I travel in this elevator before there would be an answer? Assuming that the budget could be cut and battered enough to manage a long siege, could I count on any permanent sort of answer? Or was this the beginning of a life like the elevator, up or down but seldom stabilized in one spot?

My husband looked expectantly at me, "How did your interview go, dear?"

The tears of self-pity that welled in my eyes were joined by those of sympathy for him. How many discouraged moments I had shared with him of late; how little remained even in memory of those days when my spontaneous laughter had rung out, when I had sung softly at my work, when we had shared the private jokes of those long married, when to those who knew me well, I seemed to personify "the joy of the Lord."

How could I put sparkle in my voice as I related the essentials of the interview? I tried to cling to hope. "I suppose we knew there wouldn't be shortcuts; my 'rehabilitation,' if any, will be down a long road. . . ." My voice trailed off as I thought desperately, *How long can any husband be expected to keep on pressing the cheer button for someone like me? I mustn't drag him down too; he won't be able to keep on working if he becomes depressed also.* Thus I added yet another burden to the pile I was carrying. "Cast thy burden upon the Lord" (Psalm 55:22) had always been a favorite verse, coupled with the old gospel hymns, "Take your burden to the Lord and leave it there" and, "What a friend we have in Jesus, all our sins and griefs to bear."

I realized how undisciplined my life had become. My mind whirled with opposing advice: "Sick nerves are an illness; don't try to force yourself to do anything unless you feel like it." "What you need is a job; you'd forget all about your nerves then." "Think about others; do for those worse off."

3
FORTY-EIGHT-HOUR DAYS

Through the next few days I seemed unable to face anything and quite literally turned my face to the wall. I dreaded the boys coming home from school. Neither Bruce nor Douglas was an expert in solicitude. They would come in with a "Hi, Mom," expecting a return in kind—and I could not respond. In fact, it was all I could do to force myself out of bed shortly before they were expected.

Shuffling off my bathrobe and slippers, I would slide into the dreariest dress I owned. I left my hair uncombed, my face gray and without makeup. To each I would respond in tones of impending doom, "Hello, son."

A quick look at the figure before them, and any temporary interest they showed in me would vanish. Bruce, the elder, would drop his books and head back through the front door, slamming it behind him. My muscles would shift into low gear as I hurried to the door and called after him down the long driveway.

"Where are you going, dear?"

He stopped and turned. His face seemed grim. "Well, what?"

"Where are you going?"

"Out," he said, continuing his pace. (I learned later that he had simply walked to a nearby car wash to visit a classmate.)

Bruce was not exactly a mild adolescent, and my condition seemed to make him more distant and sullen. Furthermore, my state of inner confusion made it hard to see the good qualities in him, while the poor ones were crystal clear to me.

Once during a high school football game I became terribly upset at seeing him lying injured on the grass. He was not seriously hurt, and that night he informed me that he did not want me to watch him play again. "Your nervousness bothers my friends," he said.

Douglas was inclined to put on weight, and for him our meals were a torture. I knew my cooking was mediocre, even though I expended more effort on it than normally. But night after night I would watch my younger son as he attempted to eat burnt food cooked in burning saucepans. Often there would be sharp words and he would leave the table.

Marcus was the go-between. I had the feeling that my husband started each day with a prayer for patience. Sometimes I would greet him with a word of cheer and his face would show a ray of hope. Usually, however, he took one glance and realized the worst.

The night before that Thursday interview I was awash with fears and wakeful except for a few restless, troubled dreams. Again there was the effort to dress for the interview. *I should have only one outfit and be spared decisions about what to wear,* I thought wryly. *Everything I own needs to be a different length, and I couldn't care less.*

As Marcus let me off at the busy intersection, I turned to him with sudden prescience. "I think I'm going to get my 'walking papers' from this doctor today. Whatever my day is, I hope yours is better."

Again I waited for the current interview to end; as the door opened I could hear the patient using technical terms in rather loud tones. What a gift the psychiatrist must have developed for easing them ("us," I thought with a start) out the door without offending too sensitive selves. The man who came out looked brusque and disturbed! He gave no indication of seeing my tentative smile.

The doctor greeted me and said, "It will be a few moments." He seemed more friendly, or was it just that now I knew who and what to expect and had a few crumbs of hope?

When he summoned me, he smiled in a pleasant manner; I hadn't just imagined it then. Relaxing slightly, I pulled a page of notes from my purse. I wanted to remember certain things that seemed essential to me. He asked a question or two, then left the trend of the interview up to me.

I looked at him ruefully. "Doctor, the clichés are all true. For instance, 'we get out of life what we put into it.' I have made a sad discovery; I'm afraid I haven't put into life at all what I thought I had. I'm not even the kind of person I thought I was. I pictured myself as decisive, independent. The truth is that I make an issue over the small things, but give in on all the big ones. I'm very dependent, actually indecisive, and the issues I do decide hastily are usually rash, I think now as I review my adult life. I'm appalled at what I've become— cringing, self-centered, fearful. All the interests and hobbies I cultivated for the later years have gone stale. I can't think of a thing I want to do or a place I want to go, or a relationship I want to face. Yet when I'm 'up,' I'm interested in everything. In my heart I believe that 'his strength is made perfect in weakness' (2 Corinthians 12:9), that my *feelings* do not change God's *facts* in my life; yet I seem unable to derive comfort or to rise above my own preoccupied misery."

Part of the success of the modern psychiatrist seemed to be his ability to appear sympathetic while saying almost nothing, to project an attitude of complete attention, to give the speaker a feeling of at least temporary importance, of being listened to, even at a price.

Toward the end of the interview, Dr. Bergman looked at me with real kindness as he laid down the pad upon which he had been writing. "Mrs. Fraser," he began, " 'talking it out' is the brand of psychotherapy that I employ most. After meeting with you these two times, I don't think this will help you." (I hadn't felt so either.) Nevertheless, now that my premonition of "dismissal" was coming true, I felt frightened, bereft. Where should I turn now? I agreed with my doctor that I must have some sort of professional help. I had continued to "search the Scriptures" but the habit of worry had become too much for me. My faith would have to be retrained, too. *I must listen to what the psychiatrist was saying; what had I missed already?*

My mind grasped the words, "And so I believe that definite medication is indicated. You will need to be patient; you may have to try several." *That's where I came in*, I thought wretchedly, *I've been a guinea pig for three or four prescriptions even now, none of which seemed to help.*

Dr. Bergman continued, "Therefore, I am going to refer you to another psychiatrist who specializes in medication. You understand that we do not want to make you dependent on drugs. You realize that life is not easy for anyone; no drug can make it so, but the correct medication could help you to avoid the extreme ups and downs and to adjust better.

"You have thought through your problems, perhaps for years; you know your situation well and have some pretty firm convictions

23

spiritually and otherwise. Talking would be a process like trying to chip granite with a piece of limestone. However, there is a good deal of hope that proper medication will help you."

My sense of worry sprang to the forefront at once, "But I'm afraid of many of these wonder drugs; I've heard of so many bad aftereffects."

He smiled kindly. "There is a chance in everything we do, Mrs. Fraser, but it is reasonable to assume that these drugs have been more than adequately tested. I think they will help you."

I looked at him anxiously. "Will I have to go through all this again with the new doctor? I'm so tired of talking about it."

He was reassuring. "Oh, no, I can summarize in ten minutes what it has taken you two hours to tell me."

I felt more inefficient than ever, but he was smiling so pleasantly that I ventured a flippant remark to bolster my sagging spirits. "I bet you're glad to get me off your files in a hurry, Dr. Bergman. I would be!"

I liked him tremendously as he answered gravely, "If I feel I can't be helpful, I want to see you go elsewhere." This was more than kindness; it was highly ethical. He promised to contact the other doctor as soon as possible, then we shook hands and said good-bye.

It was not until I was back on the street that I realized another avenue of escape had been blocked off. Would there be left only an interview between despair and me, a face-to-face encounter with myself as I was, or would God permit a human agency to help me?

The next day would go on record as the worst in my life. Panic swept over me. To all that I seemed unable to face were added other concerns. The financial ones I cast aside. But the failing report from my younger son's school caused me acute anguish; how much was my own condition to blame? How could I expect my sons to manage their lives well when mine was failing so miserably? How could I indicate to them what should be turned over to God's wisdom, and for what they themselves should be responsible? As for my husband— poor, poor man!

The telephone rang. It was Dr. Bergman telling me that the psychiatrist whom he had recommended was out of town but would return the next week.

Somehow I got through the endless days and nights, hating myself for counting so greatly on what mere medicine or a new "listener" might accomplish. Perhaps, though, it would add to my "will to will"; after all, if I were completely normal and well, I would be doing my work voluntarily.

I accompanied Marcus and the boys to Sunday School and church, although the messages seemed to come from afar. Yet there was comfort in the familiar sounds and phrases, and I prayed for help. My self-centered outlook frightened me more than anything. I had always been concerned about others, but when I had been alone—and I was a great deal—I was good company for myself. Now that had been stripped away. Was there some great spiritual truth that God could reveal to me only through this fearful suffering? If so, what was it? Where had I failed him? Was it in private devotions? Had I starved him out of my personal life, betrayed by the busyness of twentieth-century existence?

I began to "search the Scriptures" (John 5:39) as I had done with varied intensity throughout my adult life, but not with disciplined regularity, I realized. Avidly I began to read *The Nervous Christian* by a Christian psychiatrist who reassured me about seeking professional help in addition to belief in the Lord's power. I reread Dale Carnegie's book *How to Quit Worrying and Start Living*, semi-professional books like *How to Relax from Nervous Tension* by a Dr. Link, and so on. But most of all, I read the Psalms of David. *He* had known despair and sorrow; he spoke to my needs in a very special way.

During the week after Dr. Bergman's dismissal, every day and night had forty-eight hours. Eventually they were lived through, and my trembling fingers were dialing Dr. Van Tyl, the psychiatrist recommended by Dr. Bergman.

His receptionist was professionally pleasant. "Yes, doctor is back . . . Oh, no, nothing available in a new appointment for at least a month."

Huskily I thanked her, hung up the phone and tottered into the nearest chair.

Dear Lord, what now? I could not endure much more.

When Marcus came in from his office, I tried to rally: "Hi, honey. I haven't really been run over by a tractor; I just look and feel as if I have been."

Marcus really rallied. "Tell me all about it. There must be some way out or through it." When I'd finished, he reached for the phone and dialed a doctor friend of ours who promised to contact some of his medical acquaintances for referral to a psychiatrist.

Our friend phoned the next day and said, "I wanted to be thorough so I consulted enough doctors to learn that they all spoke very highly of Dr. Van Tyl, who is gradually taking over the practice of an older psychiatrist."

Finally Dr. Van Tyl returned my call and spoke with gentle consideration of my difficulties. I learned that mine was not a unique problem. "I have patients whose cycle changes abruptly, even day to day, and they have been helped by medication," he told me. Then came the sentence that rolled away a mountain of misery. "It sounds to me like faulty metabolism, which can be greatly helped by medication. The difficulty is to find time to see you; my appointment book is so full that it scares

27

even me to look at it, but I'll try to work you in soon. I do a great deal of institutional and court work, but I will have the nurse call you as soon as possible."

I needn't think about turning myself in to the nearest mental ward? It was after all basically a physical problem? How many otherwise well-informed people like me were aware of this possibility? How God must grieve over a world in which half of his creatures are starving, and another large share are lined up waiting to see the psychiatrist.

Was this Satan's most subtle tool against the Christian—not to take away his salvation, which the devil could not do, but to harm the witness and the joy? Was all of this current delay part of what God was trying to teach me—to "rest in the Lord, and wait patiently for him?" (Psalm 37:7)?

4
THE "BIG D"— DEPRESSION

While I was waiting and hoping for Dr. Van Tyl's office to call, I decided to jot down some reactions. Everything is one big slowdown. The smallest task seems mountainous, something to be put off as long as possible.

Other patients have told me that they feel as if the whole world were sitting on their chests, literally and figuratively. The cliché that "no news is good news" does not apply to us, for everything (we feel) is sure to be bad news whether we hear about it or not.

There is one notable exception—the Good News of the Christian gospel can remain true in the ill believer's heart; but often there is a strange sense of unreality, an inability to grasp the comfort that awaits one from its application.

Conversation becomes a tremendous effort. I who am not garrulous, but a few notches below, can think of absolutely nothing to say if I am forced to socialize at this time. I panic inwardly if I have to answer the door or the telephone.

I can just hear someone ask, "Why doesn't she forget herself and think about someone else?"

The deeply depressed person carries a burden that is hard to explain. He is convinced that he should never have been born. Sometimes he has to fight the added horror of suicidal despondency. He may be deterred from self-destruction because he did think about someone else—his family and friends, even the effect on newspaper readers who might never have known him.

Among depression patients with whom I have become acquainted are devoted parents, club women, people in Christian work, a brilliant young Jewish scholar, a wide array who cared about others but for a time were unable to cope with their own conditions.

Another evidence of the slowdown period is one's inability to write. By that I mean the inability to compose literature or personal letters, including the manual act of forming the words. Sometimes I resort to printing. When I am in that blissful state I like to call normal, I can dash off a cheery letter that is quite likely to be answered by return mail with the remark, "It was just like a good visit with you; I could actually see you saying the words as I read them."

But let me try to write a business or social

letter when I am depressed! I have been known to take days to complete a one-page letter. And then after I wearily walk to the postbox, knowing that I needed fresh air, I would stand uncertain and tortured with doubts, hesitating to drop it in, yet even more fearful that someone on the residential street would be watching and think me "queer." The minute the letter plopped inside the box, I would be harrowed. "I shouldn't have mailed it," I would say, possibly aloud. Even writing a check and addressing an envelope calls for much more energy and clear thinking than I possess at such times. I have learned to put aside the personal mail unless it is urgent, and to leave all the business mail to my husband, unless there is a deadline during his absence. If I am uncertain about an important letter that I must write, I try to seek his opinion. If he approves, I am spared the actual anguish caused by sealing the envelope.

If this seems farfetched and absurd to you, I would say, "Pause to give thanks to God that you have been spared this illness, and if you have relatives or friends thus afflicted, look at them with eyes, not of pity, but of understanding and patience, and most of all with love."

Day and night are forever when one is depressed, especially those predawn hours when it seems impossible to come up with a single cheery thought. I love to laugh, and I must admit that I derive considerable fun from making others laugh. Perhaps that is why the non-laugh, nonsmile phase is especially hard for me to bear. For the sake of my husband and my sons, for whom these varied cycles are difficult too, I am learning to pull a little cord in my brain that causes a tiny voice to say, "Smile." The first time I was sure my face had cracked, but each succeeding time the gesture is easier and the atmosphere in our home creates a new aura of hope.

Have I really made clear what depression is? From what I have written, would a well-adjusted partner in a marriage truly understand what the other (depressed) person is enduring?

If there is such a thing as a sour ice cream sundae, with a blob of whipped cream topping, also sour, I would say that describes my depressed state perfectly. Back of the woes is hidden a concentrated globule of insecurity. Nothing and nobody are without fault, but to a depressed person his own defects are the worst of all. They are such that he is sure his dear ones can't love him any more.

The mental anguish is usually accompanied by a succession of physical miseries. Perhaps they are psychosomatic; perhaps they are real. Who knows for sure? They vary from migraine to acid indigestion to aching joints and muscles. Many patients run the gamut.

Years ago my mother and I went on a liquid diet for a week or more. It was supposed to do great things for our systems. Perhaps it did. All I recall is that after taking only orange juice, plus a bouillon cube at night, for the prescribed time we finally sat down to our first meal. It was a poached egg plus a sliver of toast. I have been privileged to eat some gourmet dishes, but nothing could equal that feast. Waking up with one's depression gone is a similar experience.

5
SYMPTOMS
AND SYNONYMS

Some people have evinced curiosity—perhaps concern is a better word—about my illness. What are the symptoms? they ask. I am very tired of the symptoms; I live them much of the time. Let me share with you some synonyms for depression:

Discouragement, dejection, grief, heaviness of spirit, cheerlessness, lugubriousness, hopelessness, disconsolateness, dolor, dispiritedness, disheartenment, blues, melancholia, hypochondria, downheartedness, despondency, dolefulness, gloom, woefulness, ruefulness, gloominess, dumps, low-spiritedness, vapors, doldrums, oppression, unhappiness, lowness, sorrow, dreariness, distress, despair, desolation, misery, bleakness, sadness, darkness.

If my description of depression needed any filling out, this should do it.

I have thought of a simple illustration for

inquirers. I am a cake mix into which the cook has put too much baking powder so that I rise over the sides of the baking pan, refusing to be contained, too high and flocculent for good eating.

Or, 1 am a cake into which too little baking powder has been placed, and I respond by being flat, soggy, inedible. Now since there are good ingredients in the cake mix, the baker wants it to be just right. That is exactly what my doctor wants, and if the "cake" is a bit better each time, with a poor one at longer intervals, then he and I can look at each other with some encouragement in our eyes.

Sometimes I feel like Goldilocks in her multiple choice situation so long ago. Her aim was to feel just right, too. I doubt if I can expect to be stabilized all of the time, but the trick is to recognize mood swings and plan the days accordingly. A surprising amount can be accomplished that way.

For instance, if I have a stinging, sopping hot flash (usually when I'm in a select group) I might just as well hang out the "Welcome Depression" sign. It will descend on me within twenty-four hours. By then I may be deep into phase two, which is very simple; I just sleep night and day for most of seventy-two hours. It is interrupted only by cooking—if I have to—and eating. Whether I'm in the best company or watching the best TV show, I can't stay awake.

Why do I sleep for three days and nights? Because I'm short on the stuff. Remember I have just finished a tour of duty in high gear. My working days have been anywhere from eighteen to twenty hours a day. "Foolish," you say. Well, of course. I would like to be in bed sleeping eight hours a night, but if I'm so revved up I can't, isn't it better to accomplish a lot in my writing, or catching up on the housework? You see, that was neglected during my off-season, and I do have some concern about doing my share.

My husband is generous to help, but I think he has plenty on his mind. Even a token share from me is some encouragement to him—and to me. Our two sons are into all kinds of youth activities that seem to occupy their days fully. They are sympathetic in a detached sort of way, without really understanding the problem at all.

Call it elation and depression, the ups and downs, or just the seesaw—it's still the same old wretched manic performance. Asked to describe it on various occasions, I have tried to stand apart and look at myself and others objectively, since a similar situation might descend on them sometime. It surely attacked me with very little warning. Until the medics finally diagnosed the ailment, I thought that the Grim Reaper had come by, swinging his scythe and had sliced off the best of me, leaving just enough to keep me barely alive.

During a depression one is swathed in apathy. Nothing seems edible. Because of inability to eat, I lose eight or ten pounds with each bout. Everything is negative; there is no joy to be found in family, friends, music, TV, work, nature, reading, exercise, church, or whatever else might give happiness in better days. I have been an avid collector, but when girded in the glums, I literally shake about these treasures. I see how I have burdened our lives with things, whether by my own doing or by inheritance. But I am far enough along this lonesome trail now to know that there will be an "up" time again when these items may hold beauty for me afresh.

Meanwhile, meet Dreary Dora. One of my most embarrassing foibles concerns bath water. Normally I revel in a full hot tub, with scented bubbles aplenty. Not now. I use less and less, finally getting to a sponge bath.

Dressing is another problem. During one high spell I bought six bargain outfits. (I have learned that the only way to curb that tendency is to stay away from the shops, not even reading their ads, until the feeling goes away.) I have been known to wait until a few minutes before my husband was expected home before removing my robe and nightgown. Often the ensuing struggle to choose a dress, undies and hose has been so great that I would be saturated by perspiration and could scarcely pull my clothes on. A friend with this illness told me that once it took her twenty minutes to draw on the second stocking.

Usually we are bright people, if you will pardon the expression. This makes the path even thornier, for unless extremely manic we are aware of our thoughts and actions but scarcely able to curb them.

With all the slowdown, the patient may one day find himself in a state of extreme perturbation—walking the floor, talking aloud to himself, speaking to others with a stammering hesitancy and very little coherence. "This is ridiculous; *I* can't be acting this way," he may say, aware for the moment of his behavior. "I'll accomplish something, anything." Perhaps he starts a task; soon he is liable to sink back on the davenport and whimper, "Oh, let me sleep, dear Lord."

My doctor no longer needs to caution me about driving when I am dispirited. I am afraid to drive then, especially after dark. I doubt my coordination and my reflexes.

Yes, we are pitiful, but I repeat: we do not want pity; we crave love and understanding. Is it so much to ask?

6
HERE WE GO AGAIN

I waited another ten days, some of which were pretty bad, but I crept along clinging to the idea that hope was at least within hearsay. Several times I swallowed my natural reticence about pestering the office nurse and called to tell her again that the doctor had said he would not need to see me for long.

She was kind, but adamant—the schedule was airtight thus far. She had my name down and would keep in touch.

The next few days were a game of cat and mouse with the doctor's staff. My reactions ranged from hope and impatience to another period of deep depression. I hoped that this doctor was on the right track. After all, my close friends and relatives, even my own good sense, had pooh-poohed the idea that this was a mental breakdown. I felt agitated and discouraged that I must go on suffering just because Dr. Van Tyl had no time to see me. It seemed such a small thing to get the summary from the previous doctor and to see me briefly so that medication could be prescribed. Yet how many other would-be patients in this great city felt the same? "I wish I could help them, but I can't. I have to try to help me," I said aloud.

Did the doctor realize that I had been walking the floor with nerves atingle, that it took grit-toothed patience to endure my older son's portable radio, blaring out its din of popular music—popular with teen-agers at any rate! My husband and I had discussed our younger son's less-than-mediocre grades, and the eternal matter of the family car with two youthful, new license holders, and there had been a semblance of a family conclave. At least this gave me a feeling of being once more a working member of the family, rather than a poor creature to be pitied and endured by males who tried to understand but who found my inability to be jocose difficult going. *They* found it difficult? *I* found it almost intolerable, especially with the feeling that only a few minutes with the right doctor might help me back to health.

The days dragged by . . . a week . . . another weekend. Suddenly I could stand it no longer. I dreaded the professional tones of the receptionist, but even if it meant being a nuisance, there was a strange impulse to phone at once. I had learned to listen to these inner urges; I called them "guidance" and often thanked God for my overworked guardian angel.

Suddenly I felt deflated. "There isn't any use," I told myself. "The office nurse must be sick of the sound of my voice, and she promised to call as soon as there was the slightest leeway in the doctor's schedule."

My sense of immediacy would not be denied. Nervously I dialed, my finger slipping so that I had to hang up and try again. The line was busy. "There," I told myself, "you weren't supposed to call at all and this proves it."

But myself answered right back, "You mean to say that you expected a man as busy as Dr. Van Tyl wouldn't have a busy phone? Ring again." This argument was beginning to be wearing, so I dialed once more. This time the office nurse sounded surprised. "How strange, Mrs. Fraser. I was just noticing your name on this list of patients waiting for a cancellation. One came in a few minutes ago but I hadn't had a chance to call anyone. There are a number of people on the list, but . . . well, could you be in here at 3:30 this afternoon?"

Some might attribute my success to desperation and persistence, or even to ESP. I prefer to think that God is a God of mercy.

"Could I?" I fairly caroled to her. "I'd be there if I had to crawl on my hands and knees all the way downtown!"

She laughed at my obvious relief. "Well, 3:30 then. You might come in a little early. Good-bye for now, Mrs. Fraser." How pleasant she sounded . . . .

I would have several hours to get ready; my husband was out of town overnight, so I had the car. I would take a tepid bath, prepare slowly and carefully, and perhaps the beastly hot flashes would leave me alone today. It was cold—December—and if I weren't hurried or late . . . One of my worst sins, even when well, was not allowing enough time and then experiencing a last-minute panic.

"At least I know the office location," I thought as I maneuvered my car along the four-lane highway into the city. Marc's advice, "Take a deep breath," came to me, and I tried to inhale deeply as I drove past the lake with its iceboats sailing like huge swans, taking advantage of the strong winds. I began to feel more light-hearted than in months.

Then trouble started. I had made excellent time driving in from the suburb, but there was not a parking space in sight. What a maze of one-way streets and "no-left turns." By this time I was beginning to perspire. Where were all the outdoor parking lots? The ones I passed had "SORRY, FULL" signs at the entrances. What would I do? I found one several blocks from the clinic, but no matter, I would have to run. The wind whipped at my frame; I would have a stiff neck tomorrow. Wind and I are old enemies. But what matter whether my neck would swivel after today? If I missed this appointment, I would have little use for my neck or what was above it.

And what if I couldn't turn my neck? It would be just as well, I thought ruefully. I'd done too much looking backward during this year. I wondered if well people realized that every moment seemed an hour to one depressed.

Yet when I was well the days were not long enough for the things I wanted to accomplish. My church, my family, and my many interests encroached upon each other, vying for my happy attention. How far away that phase of life seemed now. And yet . . . was it in sight again? My hot flash subsided as I finally reached the doctor's building, but I had to mop my face as I waited for the elevator. I was reminded of a friend, a bit older than I, who went through menopause with her face streaming wet most of the time. "How could you stand dripping everywhere?" I asked in wonderment and sympathy.

"Sarah, I made up my mind that I wouldn't stay home and I definitely would not sop at my face and neck constantly. I would be a new style 'drip.'"

Bravo for that type of pioneering courage. I didn't have it. Oh, heavenly day, would the elevator never come? I could be within seconds of the appointment time if there would ever be an "up" instead of a "down" cage.

I arrived in the doctor's office three minutes

before my appointment was due. The nurse had said to come a bit early. Silly thing, why wasn't I able to schedule my time more wisely and not get in such a dither? I reported my arrival to the nurse-receptionist. I was prepared to like her. She might have been thirty-five or so; a blonde lady whose prettiness went well with her voice. She checked my name on a list and continued a jolly phone chat with a nurse in another office. They discussed a referral and injected several personal bits about their evening's entertainment. I realized they couldn't stand the barrage of misery without the lighter touch.

Looking around the room, I found it much larger than the previous office suite I had visited. From the names on the door, I deduced that Dr. Van Tyl had several partners. I hoped that some of the numerous occupants of the reception room were waiting to see the other doctors, or had brought someone there. Surely they could not all be patients.

They weren't. One anxious-appearing older couple spoke quietly to a girl who came from the inner hallway. "Did you have the brain-wave test?"

"Not yet," the attractive girl replied. Her head was immobilized in a round collar of metal and felt, indicating possibly a broken neck. She walked up to the desk and spoke quietly to the nurse who began to shuffle some cards, saying, "Let's see, yours was accident, wasn't it?'' The girl said "yes" in a low voice and turned to sit next to her parents.

I tried not to stare. Had this girl been out with a careless crowd of young people and now would have her young life permanently scarred because of a few unguarded moments? Or had a drunken driver crossed her pathway? The girl looked up, caught, and returned my sympathetic smile. "I'm going to pray that her brain isn't injured and that her neck will heal," I thought.

Idly I wondered if "hurry up and wait" was still a key saying in the Armed Forces. The minutes had stretched into an hour. It was a good thing I was in a parking lot. My nerves were misbehaving again. I had studied the pleasant realistic pictures, the warm tones of the walls—such a contrast to the gray surroundings of the other psychiatrist.

As the waiting lengthened, I found myself growing quite frightened as if this were the last chance for me. If Dr. Van Tyl didn't help me, what then? I reminded myself that the previous doctor had said that medication would help, that I need not be doomed to a life of one extreme or the other, with the depressed times increasingly long and the "up" times shorter and more hectic. He had said that there were combinations of drugs that would help me; a doctor just had to find the right ones.

"Breathe deeply," I told myself. "I must go into this interview with confidence and trust."

Tick, tick, tick. Had I been in Dr. Van Tyl's office for hours or minutes? I began to fret that I wouldn't see him in time to get my prescriptions filled that same day. After a year of misery, one would think another day wouldn't matter, but it did . . . dreadfully. If my suffering could help someone else and be salvaged as a useful experience, I felt I could bear it; still I yearned to swallow the first medication that very day.

"Mrs. Fraser, right this way. Doctor will see you now." I hoped the nurse and the others in the room hadn't noticed my nervous jump halfway from the chair when my name was called. Like a self-conscious child, I continued to raise myself as if that were the way I always got up from a chair.

I followed the nurse past a series of small consulting rooms, going into the one she indicated for me. More waiting. I ought to have brought along a book; one always had to wait in the inner office. I should have recalled this, in view of the time I had spent thus in these past months. If only it might be for some positive results.

My natural interest in others asserted itself as I studied the bookshelves crowded with medical literature, the general aura of untidy busyness. It was quite different from the pristine quarters of the first psychiatrist. Papers and files and folders were everywhere.

Presently a medium built, youngish man with

smooth black hair and intense blue eyes came briskly into the small office. "Mrs. Fraser?"

I was startled; his voice had sounded much older over the phone. Oh, my, was he really capable of understanding the subtle tortures of a middle-aged female . . . but he must be, to have such a heavy case load.

He began to question me. Did this mean he hadn't called the other psychiatrist for the ten-minute briefing? It seemed he hadn't. Well, here we go again. I must try to decide again what are the highlights. Repetition seemed so painful. He jotted down a few things, nothing so complete as the other man's notes. He was interrupted by a phone call and reached for heavy dark-rimmed glasses as he wrote down an address and date.

"That ought to be a good court fight," he spoke into the phone. "Will you be there, too? I'm not for committal myself."

Waiting, I felt grateful. This busy man, doing so much good, cared enough for me as a suffering human being to add me to his already overtaxed schedule. My confidence in him expanded. He could have his youthful look; he needed it for his pace. Besides, if he helped me, I hoped he'd live forever!

After another question or two, he wrote down two prescriptions and handed them to me as we both rose.

"Call me in ten days, after you've tried these," he told me.

I felt almost giddy with relief and expectancy. I was on my way; I just knew it! Then I glanced at the prescriptions. My heart sank and my body followed suit in the chair I had just vacated. My tones came from the depths of disappointment.

"Dr. Van Tyl," I said in a shaking voice, "I've a whole bottle full of this at home. It was prescribed by a doctor in our former home state. I quit taking it on my own, for it didn't help at all. I've had the other too, some time ago." My voice must have been dulled, distressed. So quickly hope was gone; Dr. Van Tyl had seemed my "last chance" apart from God's sending a miraculous healing.

"Well," he said soothingly, "let's try them together and see what happens. I'm afraid you're a little impatient, Mrs. Fraser."

What a deep voice he had, reassuring, too. "But doctor," I protested in self-defense. "It's been such a long year."

"I know." Somehow I felt he really did. This was rapport between physician and patient; ages didn't matter after all.

"Sometimes we're lucky and get the right combination at once. Sometimes it takes a little patience; it's not easy to balance the body chemistry."

"Not when it's misbehaved this long, I'm sure. Thank you, doctor," and even I sensed that my voice held hope again.

The improvement didn't come in a day, nor

was it perceptible to anyone in a week, but the second week I began to tackle the pile of mending. How anxious I had been to own the new sewing machine that had mocked me with its idleness almost ever since my husband bought it for me.

Our older son noticed a change. "Gee, Dad," he told his father one night during the third week, "Mother said, 'Oh, *rapt*-yure,' today. You know the funny way she used to say it when something pleased her a lot? I think she's better."

"So do I, son," said his father happily.

I had come through the doorway in time to hear the latter part of their conversation. "Praise the Lord, I think so too," I exclaimed.

Through the ensuing weeks my biochemistry did not continue to escalate. Not really. True, I had made it from the basement to the first floor, but there were several higher floors to which I could not go. In a matter of months I returned to the basement.

Had I been able to climb, this would have been a much shorter book. I'm not sure that anyone knew what had happened. There were some personal worries and shocks, but I had never had an easy life, and I thought I had learned how to accept or to fight back, depending on the urgency at hand.

It was almost impossible to reach Dr. Van Tyl, though his nurse assured me that my name was on a list for him to call at night from home.

Poor man, at times there were thirty or more names on the memo. When at last he did call, he was most gracious and unhurried, which I appreciated. I realized that he was much too busy to have taken me as a patient, but now that he had, he would strive to help me, limited as his time was.

This was the period when I discarded my name, Sarah, and said, "Just call me G. P. Fraser."

"Ha! Guinea Pig," snorted my smart menfolk. How right they were. Dr. Van Tyl and I embarked on a series of medications by telephone that is too unbelievable to record. Combinations, new medications, an endless and expensive array. Results? Negative. I might as well have swallowed sodamint tablets.

One day after backing and filling in front of the phone for over an hour, I finally made myself dial Dr. Van Tyl's office. The nurse must have sensed my desperation; she said sympathetically, "Doctor's busy with a patient, Mrs. Fraser, but hang on; I'll put you through to him very soon."

Dr. Van Tyl's beautiful voice radiated good cheer. "Mrs. Fraser, I was thinking of you today. One of my patients, a professor at the university, has been trying a new product. He danced out of my office today with the remark that he felt so great it almost frightened him. Are you interested?"

"Not in the professor, but in his pills. Oh,

my, yes," I essayed a wee joke.

Hope may spring eternal, but mine had been sprung so many times that I wondered if the spring was sprung for keeps. Still I was ready to try yet again. Tally-ho!

7
DOWN THE
DARK CORRIDOR

A tiny miracle then twinkled on my horizon. For a short time I was better. Was it due to psychological causes—"I have a fine psychiatrist," though I had to add, "if he ever has a moment to see me." Or was it because I had reached finally a phase in the cycle where I would be better anyway? I didn't know. Who did?

I seldom could see the busy Dr. Van Tyl, but he was kind enough to prescribe for me by phone several times when he could not give me an appointment.

"You say that the previous medication doesn't seem to help, Mrs. Fraser? Now this has just come on the market . . ."

"That might be the miracle drug I've been waiting for," I would answer hopefully. "Thank you for calling the pharmacy."

Aside from the anguish we cyclothymic personalities endure, there is also the drug bill. I must have taken fifty dollars' worth of the latest prescription before it was evident to Dr. Van

Tyl and to me that it wasn't going to work for me at all.

For several years I tried everything that was suggested to me. Sometimes I was better for a short while, but those times became noticeably shorter and the depressed periods longer.

I was now at the moaning, floor-walking stage when I was alone. When Marcus came home, I exercised a very tight rein on myself, but it was so difficult I would creep off to bed as soon as the dinner work was done, sometimes before.

Marcus looked at me keenly. When you've celebrated your silver wedding anniversary it's not so easy to hoodwink your mate. He said, "Have you called Dr. Van Tyl lately? I think you're worse . . . Well, have you?"

It was such an effort to answer about anything, let alone such a dreary subject as this. I felt as if my vocal chords were wrapped in cotton batting, but I tried to speak loudly enough to be heard. "Yes—well, no, I haven't. He's been away."

"But he's back now?" persisted Marcus.

"I suppose so, but what's the use? He wouldn't have time to see me. I bet that half of his case load needs to see him and can't."

Marcus snapped, "I couldn't care less about his case load. I care about you! If he accepted you in the first place, he is duty bound to see you, to try to help you, or to dismiss you. Will you promise to call him tomorrow?"

I straightened my sagging shoulders and whispered, "Yes."

Perhaps the receptionist recognized the desperation in my tone. At any rate, she put me through to Dr. Van Tyl.

A good psychiatrist can tell by a patient's voice over the phone whether he is better, worse, or at a standstill. Very early in our conversation, the doctor said, "Mrs. Fraser, it's evident that you should come into the office right away."

Glory be! I thought.

He went on, "I will be tied up mostly in court for the next several weeks and you need immediate help. You should not have to suffer without some attempt to alleviate your symptoms. Now I make this suggestion. We have just acquired the services of a fine young psychiatrist who could take you at once."

I'll bet he has no customers yet, I thought sourly and added aloud, "Dr. Van Tyl, I don't want to be difficult and stubborn, but I simply cannot go through all of my dreary history with yet another psychiatrist."

Dr. Van Tyl's deep voice softened as he said, almost wheedling, "Now, Mrs. Fraser, your husband has times when he can't assume all his responsibilities, but has to relegate some to his assistant. Doesn't he?"

"Yes, but . . ."

He continued, "You don't want to go through another extended period of misery, now do you? Let me switch you back to Mrs. White and she'll set up an appointment, then I will see you as soon as I can. All right?"

Nothing in the world was all right, but I had been brought up in that lovely era of good manners, so I said, "Yes, thank you for talking with me, doctor."

It took my weary brain some time to realize that I wouldn't have to tell young Dr. Williams a thing. My file was right across the hall in Dr. Van Tyl's suite.

The time was December and our city, like many across the country, already showed the effects of a hard winter. Marcus, thinking to help me, left the car for me to drive to my appointment. The ice and snow and my own slowed reactions made it a frightening expedition. But the new doctor proved personable, sensitive, and kind. It was a toss-up as to whether I felt sorrier for him or for myself. I truly tried to help him out—after all, he knew practically nothing about me while I, unfortunately, knew entirely too much about me.

Dr. Williams had just asked me something. What? I had no idea what . . . lift your head, look at him directly; he is here to help you. Leave your hangnail alone, stop twisting your wedding ring . . . . Was he repeating his question or was this a new one? Concentrate, listen. He is asking to be excused for a moment. Nod graciously, say, "Of course, doctor."

Time was a blur for me then. Probably he

returned in a few minutes, "Dr. Van Tyl would like to see you while you are in the office, Mrs. Fraser."

So he wasn't too busy after all to take a look at a battered old patient! I don't know what I said or answered, but it seemed I was there quite a while. He didn't say much; sixth sense whispered to me that something drastic was on its way to me.

So oppressed and depressed was I that I could not make it back to the car without pausing for a while on a bench inside a public building. How would I ever get home? The blankness of my thinking apparatus was such that it never occurred to me to telephone Marcus to come for me—his office was only a few blocks away.

He came in two or three hours later looking as close to defeat as I had seen him. "Dr. Van Tyl called me after you left his office."

"He called you? But he's never done that. What did he want?"

Marcus looked at me and sighed deeply, "He wants to put you into the hospital at once."

I started to tremble visibly; I'd been doing it internally for aeons.

Marcus continued, "He said that he had never seen you so deeply depressed. I agreed."

"Then what did the doctor say?"

"He said that you appeared to be in a suicidal depression, and I would have to take the responsibility of your welfare if you delayed going to the hospital."

"Marcus! Why would you tell me such a gruesome thing? I don't feel well enough to bear it."

"I told you because I will have to have your cooperation. I think you can be trusted, but I need your help."

Only once before had I come close to ending my life. I had saved sleeping capsules for months when I was supposed to be taking one a night. Finally I had more than enough, but I couldn't go through with it. I saw my family and I saw hell, too, for I'm a Christian and believe that God releases his own in his time, not ours. I told the Lord then, "I guess I can stand some more hell on earth if I can be sure of heaven in the here-after."

8
SHOCK WITHOUT THERAPY

So it was definite. I was to be taken to a private sanitarium a few miles out of the city. Because of suicidal tendencies associated with my type of illness, a friend came and stayed with me, and cooked dinner for the boys and Marcus. When my husband came home, I stalled for half an hour, trying to find a pair of shoes of the right color. Finally we drove off and arrived about dusk. My one contribution to the conversation en route was to repeat the word "no" over and over.

The sanitarium was an oldish building, beautifully located on a bluff overlooking a river. Marcus carried in my suitcase, and signed permission for me to be given electroconvulsive therapy. I had to sign too and once again I balked, but finally I added my name to his.

For me the treatments were a nightmare. A thick rubber collar was inserted into my mouth and a wire was attached to my head. There was a horrid, unforgettable thrill before I blacked out. Today, I understand, shock patients are given Sodium Pentathol and encounter none of the sensations I have described.

I have known other patients who responded almost miraculously to shock therapy. Others have had to return for additional treatments. I received ten treatments over five weeks, but their therapeutic value was nil, and today I can remember practically nothing that took place during that time. I was astonished to learn that Marcus drove out to see me every night, and that several friends called and spent hours with me on weekends.

"Don't you remember at all, honey?" Marcus asked me months later, a trace of sadness in his voice.

I pondered my reply. "Mostly I remember sitting in the sun with somebody and watching the leaves twirling toward the ground. Then I remember that the wind would set the leaves to dancing. I could never stand the wind, but this was a warm, caressing breeze. Did I eat in the dining room? It seems that I did, and that there was a man at our table who annoyed me."

Marcus chuckled. "Your memory is coming back, praise the Lord," he said. "You're quite right, the man was sarcastic; you mentioned it at the time." I was so grateful.

"It's coming back," I said. "I remember that man. He was a doctor patient, about forty years old. He made me want to go back to isolation for my meals. And I remember, too, that there was a large old house nearby that had been remodeled for occupational therapy. I walked over to look at it but didn't want to make a thing, and that was unusual, for I love crafts.

"When I got home I found a Turkish towel that had been made into a sleep shade. I probably told the therapist that I had forgotten to pack one, and she must have made it for me, bless her. I do hope I thanked her."

"You would have, I'm sure."

"Anything else to recall, or can we put this on the closet shelf and close the door forever? I don't like whole hunks shut out of my conscious mind, no matter how troubled it was. Did I maintain any spiritual contacts during those weeks?"

"Oh, yes, you went nearly every Sunday to the little white church a few blocks away."

"I did? Alone? I hope I behaved well."

"Of course you behaved well. Haven't you been a minister's wife for twenty years? Probably you could have stepped into the pulpit and preached a good sermon, if you had been asked. Do you recall the Halloween party?"

"I think so. The nurses had worked so hard cutting out paper pumpkins and making decorations. I remember trying to act as if I were having a whale of a time, though I never did care much for bobbing for apples. But the staff seemed to know that I was grateful for their efforts to relax our minds and bodies."

9
OUT OF CIRCULATION

Two years later I was admitted to the mental health ward of the metropolitan hospital, suffering from a severe recurrence of depression.

The winter was at its dreariest—ice, banks of dirty snow, dull gray clouds. I thought ruefully that it was tailored to measure for my mood. My husband kept his eyes on the road ruts and said nothing. I kept trying to wink back tears; the weather was so subzero that even my tears felt cold.

Finally I burst out, "Why have I come back to this? What has happened to me?"

Marcus tried to cheer me, reminding me that it was not punishment but a means of restoring me to health.

After I had been registered and he had carried the luggage to my room, he leaned over to kiss me good-bye. I clung to him and the tears flowed at last. "Please don't tell anyone where I am! I'm so ashamed."

He knew it was futile to try to comfort me, but he made the attempt, bless him.

That evening when I was lying listless on the bed, unable to concentrate on reading, equally unable to turn my mind from its sad meanderings, I felt a light touch on my shoulder.

"Hello, Mrs. Fraser. Are you all settled in?"

I turned over and gasped. It was a young friend. "Marty! Any other time I would love to see you, but not now, not here."

She smiled cheerfully. "Why not? I'm glad to see you or I wouldn't be here."

For the second time that day I broke into uncontrollable sobs, though I'm not really the weepy sort. "I'm so ashamed to have come back."

"Why, Mrs. Fraser, you needn't be. I've had shock therapy. There's nothing to be ashamed of."

"You have?" I blurted. I couldn't believe that this nice-appearing girl had fought the same battle. I noticed her red smock. "How did you happen to find me?"

"I've been doing volunteer work on the main desk once a week. Looking through the names of patients, I saw yours. Simple as that. I do hope I haven't upset you," she looked at me solicitously.

"Quite the contrary," I assured her. "If you are Exhibit A, I have hopes for me."

I should have known that the hospital staff wouldn't leave me to brood very long. I had sedation that night, and the next day between tests and medical business, a pleasant nurse escorted me around the crafts room. I was completely disinterested in the various projects, but I had the grace to feel embarrassed about it. She opined that I would feel "more like it" soon. While I didn't really believe her, it was something to think about. I could hardly foresee that I would become the most eager worker in O.T. (occupational therapy) and would take home numerous mementos from loom and saw.

Right here I would like to pay tribute to the occupational therapists. In addition to their skills, they are shrewd psychologists. Not one of the depressed patients wants to make anything in O.T. when he is first shown the projects. But the usefulness of occupational therapy as a restorative to mental health can hardly be overestimated. The exercises, excursions and programs play a large part in the recuperative process, I believe.

One evening a friend telephoned me. "Well!" she exclaimed, "I can't believe I've got you on the phone. I've called three times today. 'I'm sorry, Mrs. Fraser is in the exercise class.' Next time—'I'm sorry, Mrs. Fraser is at occupational therapy.' Last time—'Sorry, Mrs. Fraser has just gone bowling.' Now," said my friend, "I have just one question to ask you, How do *I* get in?"

I giggled, thinking of her busy home and church life as well as other commitments.

"The activities help," I told her, "but life in a hospital is not all that great."

There would be times when I would be

allowed none of the privileges, according to the way my biochemistry was performing.

A well-meaning person said to me several years ago, "Throw out that medicine, take long walks, rediscover bicycling, have some fun and you'll soon be fine."

I tried that once when my doctor was away and I had cancelled an appointment with his associate. The results were too dismal to mention. Be wary of the advice of even the most compassionate layman, who knows the symptoms only by sight and hearsay.

Every mental health person must learn the basics: Keep in close touch with your doctor. He may make a mistake now and then, but almost always he knows the score. (If you can't trust him, the psychiatrist would probably agree that you should say good-bye and seek help elsewhere.) Thank God that modern scientists have made great strides in the medication field.

When the depression cycle changes to elation, it is hard to bear before it becomes regulated. Suddenly I feel that there is so much to do, so many neglected chores, that I have to be very stern with myself not to fly in all directions at once. It is difficult for me to sleep enough, and I find myself not sure what day it is. If this seems odd, try a few nineteen- or twenty-hour days in succession. This is the time when I enjoy being with people, but I have to watch my husband or an intimate friend to make sure that I am not shouting or monopolizing the conversation.

Sometimes there has been a glorious interim of a few days between the up and down cycles when I have felt it was all worth-while. Then do I ever praise the Lord!

10
THE PLAYER PIANO

I referred to my first hospitalization as "The Player Piano Period." The piano was the universe; I was the roller from which came sad, sweet or devout sounds, depending upon the marks on the roll. My psychiatrists were the ones who set the music in motion by pumping. If the pedals were neglected, the music would grind to a groaning stop, the roller helpless in its place above the keyboard.

I was very sensitive to the tunes being played on me during the next weeks, when I showed a sudden swing toward normality. The doctors might well have sung Colonel Pickering's song in *My Fair Lady*, "She's got it, she's got it, by George, I think she's got it!" But I didn't have it. Very soon I went too high.

Dr. Van Tyl knew that I was scheduled to give a talk. "Better write your speech now," he warned. "I guarantee it will be a better one than you can manage next week."

My handwriting is always affected by the

highs or lows, being shaky for the latter and illegible during the former. I'm pretty sure that with the aid of the Almighty I wrote a good speech. I should have had a tape recorder. When I looked again at the speech I was skidding toward the "glummies," unable to decipher a dozen words.

By the time a new combination of medication began to take hold, it was too late for the meeting. I called the chairwoman, and she was graciousness itself. The next month's speaker was able to fill in. The experience had a happy ending for everyone except me.

Becoming depressed right before the doctor's eyes and under the nurses' noses was too much. The struggle to look, sound and feel cheerful was beyond me. When the senior doctor motioned me to a chair in the little cubicle that served as a conference room, I burst into troubled conversation. I needn't wait for him to ask how I felt; he knew by looking at me.

My lips quivered, not so much in self-pity as from weary nerves.

"Doctor," I said, "I know I am losing my mind."

Dr. Van Tyl leaned toward me and said earnestly, "Sarah" (the only time he ever called me by my first name). "Of course you're not losing your mind. You have a very good mind. It's just that you have a biochemical imbalance, and we don't know what causes it to swing one way or the other. Research chemists are working night and day and sometime they'll find the answer. Meanwhile your condition can be relieved by medication. We just have to find the right combinations."

Many hours of intermittent anguish and gaiety lay ahead, but nothing was ever so bad after that interview. The doctor had administered the greatest of all medicines. He had given me a window on the garden.

11
GRACIOUS LIVING

My stay in the metropolitan hospital stretched into nearly seven weeks during which there were several minor crises. My next roommate was a pleasant woman in her thirties who was nearly ready for dismissal. We had an amiable time except that she stayed bewildered for quite a while after her shock therapy and was inclined to deny everything that she had said or done.

A quiet two or three nights were my happy lot after she left. Then a rather hard-faced woman came in. Later I learned that she was an alcoholic. Privately the doctor assured me that she would be very quiet, under sedation. He added that I would be moved soon; both doctors felt that I was too sympathetic to the problems of the other patients for my own good, and as soon as a single room was available, I would be moved to it.

The next morning Dr. Van Tyl met me in the hall and inquired about my night. I fixed my hollow eyes on the dear man. "The sedation prescribed for my roommate must have been outdated a few years. It certainly didn't work. She spent the night tossing, moaning and swearing. As soon as I dared, I went out to the lounge. How did I sleep? Thank you for asking, but I didn't."

I was moved twice before they settled me for keeps in a single room. Since the medical aide and a nurse or two put all of my belongings on my bed and made quick work, moving the whole on castors, it wasn't as much of an upheaval as it sounds.

It was when I finally attained single status, hospital-wise, that I began my "Gracious Living" program. I kept bringing attractive brasses and curios from home. I had some things from the Holy Land, and so many visitors and patients wanted to buy them that I did a rather flourishing business. Seemed to make everybody happy, including me as I planned to give the profits to charity.

Of course the other half of the joy of selling is the fun of buying, so I was very fond of going into the hospital shop down off the lobby. All went well, though I had to have an aide in tow, but one day, alas, I went too far. I bought a pair of lovely small silver candelabra which were not cheap, but were satisfying to my aesthetic soul.

Dr. Van Tyl, while admiring them, called a halt. He made the shop off limits for me.

"But doctor," I protested, "the shop is to help the free bed patients."

"True," he tried to suppress a grin, "but even the free bed bit can be overdone."

Of course I knew he was right.

The longer I stayed, the more *objets d'art* I brought from home, when I went there on occasional passes. It is my opinion that I was helped psychologically, being surrounded by beautiful things, including two paintings. Some of the women patients dressed in old slacks or wrinkled jeans, not from poverty, but quite possibly from ennui. There have been times when I felt that I could not dress up or change frequently, but even in my worst depressions, I tried to be well-groomed and to stay away from dreary colors.

But as the weeks progressed the doctors tried one combination of pills after another, to no avail. I became too high, and then just before I was dismissed, I felt myself slipping back into discords of emotional misery—low, low, lower than any mood of normal human experience.

12
EFFECT ON THE FAMILY

Eventually my biochemical elevator came back up from the sub-basement to ground level and I was allowed to return home. Dr. Williams prescribed another change of medicine, but it failed to achieve the desired stabilization. But as Marcus reminded me rather sharply one day, "No pill can do everything. You have to help yourself." He made it clear that he did not think I was really trying. I know he was hoping that a change of tone would prove helpful, but his words simply threw me again. How could he say that the lethargy I still felt was self-imposed?

Bruce, our elder son, had entered the service and had been shipped to Vietnam. I managed to get off a letter to him every week, but I doubt that he read it. My handwriting was not the most legible, and I found it took a supreme effort to write cheerfully.

Bruce had not been an easy child to bring up, and we felt his volunteering for military duty was partly a desire to get away from home—that is, from me and my problems. It was, therefore, highly gratifying to receive a letter from camp before he went overseas, saying that he had come to appreciate his parents and the home they had provided him. We could hardly believe our eyes. Later, from Vietnam, he wrote expressing his appreciation for the chaplains whom he had come to know. This was another surprising departure from his previous attitudes.

Such moments of encouragement did not come often, for Bruce's time in combat was one of great anxiety for us. I watched the television reports from the war zone half-expecting to see Bruce, and dreading the prospect. Many times I left the room until the newscast was over; depression had a way of magnifying even the awfulness of war. Marcus told me one day that he had laid Bruce's life in the lap of the Lord. I found it hard, if not impossible, to do the same.

After Bruce returned safely from the war zone, there were a few amiable times around the house, but we noticed that he was extremely nervous. He smoked a pipe much of the time. At night we would hear him cry out in his sleep, and sometimes he would get out of bed, take the car, and drive into the country for hours.

Bruce and Douglas had never been particularly close, but now I noticed a real gap growing between them. Neither of course knew what to make of the pogo-stick changes in my illness. But for that matter, neither did I.

On one occasion Douglas, who was now in high school, visited me in the hospital. He brought with him a girl whom I did not know. At the moment I was in high elation, and was enormously pleased that he would make the effort to see me. But my efforts to act natural got out of hand; that is to say, I overdid it and became quite garrulous.

After a while I saw Douglas looking both embarrassed and annoyed. After he and his friend left, I lay there wondering what she had thought of me, and if she suspected there was "something wrong."

I suppose an accurate case history would record that both sons had contributed to the underlying causes of my condition. For that matter, so had my husband, and my early upbringing without a father, and a whole shoe box full of other precipitating factors. But trying to fix blame is a wearying and useless undertaking. My problem was not who or what caused it, but rather how to get out of it.

13
FOURTH TIME AROUND

Nineteen months had passed since my second visit to the hospital, and I was beginning to feel encouraged. Then one wintry day I pulled my little car alongside an elaborate glass building. I had never seen this structure before.

As I entered, a smiling car salesman approached.

"I feel terribly silly," I told him, "but I'm lost. I've lived here for years but don't know where I am."

He was very kind. I was astounded to discover that just across the freeway was a huge shopping center that I knew very well.

"Where did you want to go, ma'am?"

What did I tell him? I have forgotten. Whatever it was, eventually I arrived home. My husband called out anxiously, "Did you get your test all right? You were gone quite awhile."

So that was it! I must have meant to go to the hospital for my lithium level. Instead I drove miles in another direction. I gave a vague answer, not wishing to worry him further. It was evident that I had arrived home purely by divine guidance. God reached me with a message: "Don't drive again, Sarah, for any reason until you know that you are well."

The truth was that things had been getting worse instead of better. For weeks I had not stopped working at various projects. For the last three days and nights I had not even undressed. I had put in several lengthy long-distance telephone calls.

All of the extra clothes I owned were piled in the middle of the living room to be shipped to missions overseas or to be placed on sale in local thrift shops.

At three o'clock one morning, after ten minutes sleep, I thought, "I'm exhausted, but my dratted biochemistry won't let me slow down or rest. I feel like the heroine in a bad fable. I'll have to do something creative to quiet my mind. The body rest will come later." I had bought one of those imitation Christmas spruce trees and proceeded to put it together. By now I was smiling and humming under my breath. "Roses," I thought, "with the angel of the rose at the top." I had some permanent flowers in my basement workroom. After an hour or so I stepped back and surveyed my efforts. Perhaps it wasn't as charming as it seemed to me, but I felt almost reborn. I stepped up to adjust a rose petal and patted a branch. "Dear tree," I said.

Six hours later I was in hell. I was ordered into the hospital; my husband couldn't get away, so I had to call a taxi. The driver arrived before I had finished packing. He was very suspicious about some coats I wanted to carry with me. I explained that they were for some of the clean-up maids whom I knew at the mental health unit. By the soothing tones he used toward me, I knew that he was assessing whether I was just emotional, dangerously insane, or something in between. Apparently I was not his first "wild" fare.

Moments later I signed in for my fourth hospitalization, feeling a degree of self-pity. Of course my fatigued mind realized I needed professional care as soon as possible. I almost looked forward to getting off the elevator, thinking, "Here I am again; fix me up, please." But I, who had known all the nurses so well, saw not one familiar face as I walked down the well-remembered wing.

The acting head nurse was a young woman with lovely hair and classic features. When I approached she snapped into command. Instead of the welcome treatment I expected, here was a strange young woman looking at me severely, or so it seemed. Probably she wasn't harsh, but she appeared so to my overly sensitive reactions. Her demeanor had the effect of making me "stir crazy." I was to do and say things in the next hour that I would not have believed myself capable of doing.

An aide arrived with my vast array of luggage. The nurse set her jaw firmly and with a first-things-first expression hustled me to a four-bed ward. I protested, "Sometimes I have had to share a double room, but Dr. Van Tyl and Dr. Williams have always wanted me to have a single room."

It seemed none was available now. The nurse added (rather haughtily, it seemed to me), "You needn't put away your clothes yet—there may be a double room later today." I always enjoyed the company of the nurses and medical aides on this station. I felt they were part and parcel of the team that would help to make me well, bless them. This, however, was starting out differently.

When I left the house my aunt was unwell, and I was extremely concerned about her. I explained to the acting head nurse I *must* call home. She refused to let me do this. It was my first hospitalization without telephone privileges and without visitors "except my husband."

"You call her then," I pleaded. "She is just recovering from an illness, and I will never forgive myself if anything happens to her there alone." She shook her head.

My tortured mind advised, "Threaten her! Scare her. It's worth it to have Auntie called." I heard a voice that must have been mine shouting, "You let me out of here to phone my auntie or I'll kill you!"

She stood sentry-like before the door. I remember Mark Twain's story about the "awful solid dog," and fell back temporarily beaten. It occurs to me that I may not have been the first mental health patient to threaten her; her manner may have induced such behavior in others. Mercifully, in time Dr. Williams appeared. Before he had me "put to sleep" for a while, Miss Acting Head, smiling prettily in front of the doctor, reported to me that Auntie had called and all was well.

It is my recollection that I slept for three days and nights. Sleep was first on the agenda for future biochemical adjustment.

When I finally awoke I began to worry over some business matters. Again I begged the acting head nurse to let me call my aunt.

"No."

"Then will you let me speak to my lawyer?"

"No."

"My husband?"

"No." Her head was still shaking sideways, just in case I had another request. I thought she was out of bounds on that one.

Several days later I said to her grimly, "I've lost thousands of dollars by being kept incommunicado, and while I have always liked this hospital, I'm going to sue everybody in sight when I get out of here."

It was all very real and very tragic to me. I am not the threatening type. I love the Lord and I love his creatures. It was a while before I learned that there was no money lost. I felt so ashamed, so discouraged.

In a few days I was sufficiently rested to remember the clothing I had brought for the cleaning maids. I knew the coats hadn't been packed in a suitcase. Then I began to look in my closet, drawers and suitcases for some other items. By the time my husband came to call I was in a tizzy. "The clothing?" he asked. "I took it back at the nurse's request."

Feeling very unpleasant, I muttered, "More than likely she thought I was harboring stolen goods. What about my missing Bible, my books, writing materials, and family photos?"

"Perhaps they're in the package she gave me to take home."

I made a disagreeable reply, whereupon Marcus preached a little sermon on how I could not expect to get well unless I learned to cooperate with *everyone*.

I retorted, "Miss Vinegar is the first person in years that I haven't liked; I was trying to like her. Then she told me how many times she had gone through my suitcase to ascertain what things I didn't need. Wasn't that darling of her?"

"Try to cooperate, dear. I know it's hard, but it's for your benefit, too. I'll bring your Bible and the other things tomorrow." He patted my shoulder and leaned down to kiss me good-bye.

"Thanks for coming. I didn't mean to be horrid, but that . . . Oh, dear, there I go again.

Maybe by tomorrow I will dare to walk past the nurses' station to the elevator with you when you leave."

Dr. Williams apologized to me several days later. "I'm sorry I was out of town. If you could have come in even two weeks earlier, we would have caught this and you wouldn't have needed to go through such a very bad time."

"Your caring helps," I told him, "but it has been grim. If only dear Nurse Carter had been here, things would have been better, I know."

When Nurse Carter did come back after a bout of flu, I did everything but bake a cake in her honor. I told her a little of my bad time and of the lack of rapport between her substitute and me. She was satisfactorily sympathetic, but she added, "We try our best."

"I'm sure you do," I replied, "and I don't mean to add to your cares by complaining. I do want to ask one more thing though. When I begged to call my lawyer, did she have a legal right to refuse me? After all, I'm not crazy, though I know I've been very ill."

"Of course you're not crazy, Sarah. You never will be. Your mind is not affected by your biochemical illness. I would say that she did not have a right to prevent a business call since you felt it was so urgent. They would have known soon whether your concern was valid, I think. You see, though, a head nurse often has to rely on her own judgment. The doctor is not always available."

I told her, "You have a kind, second-mile

personality, bless you." I strolled down the hall leaving her to a stack of paperwork. I felt unburdened.

No single room became available, so for over three weeks I had to manage with a roommate. You might ask if she had to manage with me, but let the story unfold . . . .

She was a gentle little woman, sixty-five or so, who was having shock therapy for a mild but persistent depression that developed after the death of her somewhat domineering husband. She spoke very little.

Her children were most faithful in visiting her. I tried to give them privacy by going out to the lounge, but most of the patients there were chain-smoking. There was liable to be a cacophony of sound too—TV, record player, younger game players.

I could have sneaked over to the next wing which had a nice area for visitors and was comparatively quiet. Surgery patients and their guests used this spot. Often it was empty, except during visitors' hours. Since Nurse Carter trusted me and I was fond of her and treasured that trust, I did the right thing. Waving a hand toward the smoky buzz, I pleaded, "Could I please go over and sit in the next section?"

She had an endearing smile. "Of course, Sarah. You won't wander down to the main floor and the hospitality shop, will you?"

"I promise." I had spent a lot of money in

the shop and it was off limits to me, except with an aide, when I could buy some small articles. Good reason. There were times when I had to be protected against myself.

The surgery visiting area was quite a diverting interlude as an old gentleman in a wheelchair engaged me in conversation that seemed to cheer us both. Finally I picked up my knitting and returned to the room for my dinner tray. Possibly it was the shock therapy, but my roommate slept day and night except for meals and callers.

Every breath my sleeping roommate drew, day or night, was a solid, steady, rhythmic snore. It never deviated for one second. It wasn't a violin snore; it was strictly bass fiddle. I was becoming almost as high-geared as when I entered, then mercifully she was dismissed. She was so sweet that of course I never indicated that she had been a difficult roommate. I realized that some other types could have made life much harder to endure.

14
WAY UP THERE

What is it like when a manic-depressive patient goes into orbit? Although I have seen others with similar symptoms, I know my own best. It is hard to imagine the feeling of excitement and breathlessness that characterizes this state of being. Everything seems to click into place. One feels at peace with his Maker, the world and himself. Colors are brighter, children smarter, food tastier, housework more pleasant, friends dearer. All skills seem accentuated.

At the wheel one seems to be driving more safely and efficiently, though one is quite apt to begin accumulating traffic tickets. I remember tooling my little car ninety miles an hour on a city freeway just to see how fast it would go.

One's cheery disposition brightens the day for elevator operators, clerks, waitresses, switchboard attendants—anyone in town. There is a glad word for all, and only at the end of the day does it occur to one that he is exhausted. Insomnia deprives the patient of any real recuperation through restful slumber.

Possibly the worst outgrowth of my own experience in the "highs" has been my buying binges. A girl friend of one of my sons called me a compulsive buyer. I was pretty hurt over that, but I know she was right.

My husband said one day, "This house can't hold all you're bringing in." I put him off by saying that much of the merchandise was bought for others. Usually the purchases were clearance items and could not be returned. I forced myself to take back some impossible things. Dr. Van Tyl suggested removing my name from our mutual checkbook and confiscating my credit cards.

"That wouldn't work," I told my husband sadly. "I would just pay cash."

A cousin who has been most sympathetic said to me once, "You know, it's almost worth your severe depression to have the ecstatic time you do when you're high."

"No," I said, "nothing is worth that state of mind, but I'll admit in some ways being 'high' is super because of the rose-colored glasses I wear."

After the money is spent, of course, what had been such fun suddenly becomes bleak and frightening. I realize that I shouldn't have spent it all, and worse, that I have "squirreled" the house with a vast assortment of unnecessary things. Under the most favorable circumstances, I am a mediocre housekeeper. Now it is impossible.

We were sitting at a long table in the hospital, ready to begin our group therapy session. The discussion was about overbuying. Several commented on their problems in this regard, and one young man asked the doctor, "Is it curable? It is something we'll outgrow?"

Perhaps I only fancied that the doctor glanced in my direction. I raised my hand and he signaled for me to proceed.

"Last year," I said, "I left a clerk in a state of partial collapse when I quickly bought ten pairs of sale shoes. Then I put on weight and had to get a different size. Some good came out of the venture, for I passed the shoes along to a needy friend who said she had never owned so much footwear. Such largesse is nice, but hard on the budget. I have bought furniture when there was no place for it. Finally my husband alerted one or two shops not to sell to me without calling him first.

"You asked if it were curable. I don't think so, for I have fallen into the buying pit almost every time I have been high. I know now that I am a chronic case; the news of rummage sales, store bargains, thrift stores, all leave me panting in anticipation.

"I realized at last that my chief problem was *bargains*. I am tempted to buy only when things are on sale at reduced prices. When I am low I want nothing, and wish that most of what I own could be shoved off a cliff. But when I am high, if I walk past a hardware store where screw eyes are on sale, I'll buy 5,000!"

Everybody laughed, and the head nurse leaned over and patted my hand, saying, "Even when you're down, Sarah, you still have your sense of humor."

A woman raised her hand. "But suppose you really need something from the stores?"

"I try to go in like an arrow to the counter I need, eyes front, get what I must have and leave at once. My main problem has been to admit that I have this problem. 'It's me, O Lord, standin' in the need of prayer.'"

15
A STAR OF HOPE

I have a friend whose complexion matches the translucence of Rosenthal bone china. Her sensitivity has been for her a pitfall at times, but some of my most comforting messages have come from her. Several years ago after a nervous breakdown she was seriously considering suicide. She had youth, beauty, popularity; but she had not been able to find peace and joy. She was not sure they existed.

Some of her friends suggested that they all attend an evangelistic service "for laughs," but they reckoned without the force of the living God. The evangelist ended his sermon and gave an invitation to those who would enter upon the Christian life to step forward. The Lord's hand was laid upon my friend and she saw herself almost as an outside observer moving forward to take the first faltering steps down the Christian path.

From that point my friend's life has been radiant, though not in one easy lesson. Her witness has influenced many people, and she is frequently booked for speaking engagements. Yet her biochemistry continues to falter periodically. Depression is always hovering in the wings, seeming to do battle with her spirit.

What does this mean? That Christianity is no good? Hardly. People who suffer from this illness will tell you that one of its worst effects is a sense of loneliness and helplessness that sometimes amounts to sheer terror. When the Christian patient realizes that he is not alone, that God is right there beside him, helping him not *out of* but *through* it, the worst is over.

At one of our group therapy sessions a young business executive who had been having a rough time asked a question, and pressed the psychiatrist for an answer. "Does the patient cease in time to go through manic and depressive cycles?"

Dr. Williams replied slowly and carefully. "If it has been a one-time experience there is a good chance it will not recur. If it has already recurred several times, I would say no. But proper medication can cause the cycles to become less severe."

As the doctor spoke I sat there feeling that a piece of my heart had just died. I thought of an incident at a supermarket meat counter. Perhaps one never forgets true desperation and embarrassment, for I remember that I stood in front of the frozen turkey counter for forty-five minutes. I could *not* decide what to get.

Should I buy a small turkey, a turkey roll, or just give in and get TV turkey dinners? How could I prepare and serve any of it? First one, and then another butcher came from behind the counter asking if I were not feeling well, or could they help any way in my selection. I don't know what I muttered to them; I'm pretty sure I thanked them. It was almost closing time. I grabbed the turkey, sure that I was making the wrong selection, and made it to the checkstand.

I glanced around the table. Everyone else looked the same as they did before the gentle note of doom was pronounced. I suppose I did too. Yet I remembered that "the firmament sheweth his handiwork." God is still in control of his universe, and the star of hope is still shining. He knows whereof we are made; and he can heal as well as save.

Meanwhile we continue on with our baffling idiosyncrasies and our frail emotional balances. For some the symptoms do not recur, praise the Lord. We who are not so fortunate cannot afford the luxury of envy. We have to assess the weight of our individual burdens, adjust our mental cargo, and carry it with as much grace as God will give and as much courage as we can muster.

16
THE CARDINAL

One day I discovered within myself an utter inability to cope with reality. I had a longing for numbness and even for complete unconsciousness. I opened the door to the medicine cabinet, then shut it resolutely. Suicide was no solution to the problems that were overwhelming me. Yet it seemed there must be some course open that possessed Christian dignity and held some hope of ultimate release.

A dark voice whispered to me, "My dear, there isn't a soul who would blame you. Why, they would rush to your defense. You are hardly responsible for your actions. Think of what you have been going through. Wouldn't you like to wake up in heaven with no more woes, no more ghastly days and nights to face?"

I clutched the fixture before me to keep from swaying. A fresh wave of weakness broke over me. I moved into the bedroom and flung myself across the bed, crying out, "Oh, God, help me!"

When I awakened from sleep I arose, walked past the mirror and shuddered. Even as I looked, the features crumpled into tears. Passing into the kitchen and surveying it, I felt a fresh qualm of responsibility. There were dishes in the sink. If I were gone, who would wash them?

What of my continuing role as a lay worker and a confidante of women in trouble? What of those outside the church who were always so quick to tear Christians to pieces? Turning from the sink, I thought of the words of a chorus:

> Now I belong to Jesus,
> Jesus belongs to me.

But did I? Did he?

I had always enjoyed creative cooking, but now I found it oppressive to prepare and serve even the simplest edible food. My seasonings were "off"; things burned. I kept trying, but everything was a supreme effort.

Wearily I shifted a pile of unmended clothing from a kitchen chair. As I sat down, I lifted the familiar, black-covered Bible from among the tea and coffee cups on the table. Almost indifferently I leafed through First Corinthians until my eye caught a verse in the tenth chapter:

> There hath no temptation taken you but such as is common to . . . women!

Was it a gloss on the text or just my imagination? For the thousandth time I asked, "Is there no spiritual answer to this bottomless depression? Is it really all glands and chemistry and the merry-go-round of the pills?"

My fingers lifted the pages back to the Psalms:

> Thy word have I hid in mine heart, that I might not sin against thee (Psalm 119:11).

That was it. This illness was a sin against God. It involved something deeper than the destruction of health and the interruption of normal family life. I stood at enmity with the Almighty. These frail arms were pushing away the whole universe, yet I was so desperately lonely! And when I went to church, the words of the preachers clattered on my broken spirit as rain falling on a tin roof.

I knew my outlook was being warped by illness, but could not shake the feeling that all life and endeavor were futile. Though I tried hard to "stand on the promises," to recall my interest in the cultural arts, to think of others, I felt stifled by recurring despair. I who had been accused in the past of being voluble now found forming the simplest sentence a struggle. It seemed to me that the power of evil was effectively putting a halt to my prayer life. I, who have often led in public prayer, now could barely formulate the whisper, "Lord, I believe; help thou mine unbelief" (Mark 9:24).

Oh, I knew the words of the Christian message, but what had happened to the music? Was this depression of the devil? Was it true that at one time I had committed my way unto the Lord, and acknowledged him so that he could direct my paths? If that were true, where was he?

It was at this point in my introspection that I looked out the kitchen window and saw a cardinal and its mate perched on a lilac bush. I could not believe it; all we had seen for weeks past were starlings and crows. I reveled in the gorgeous scarlet coloring of the male, the soft hues of the female. The male sang his clear, strong call. Here was a joyful and lovely bit of nature, something cheerful to relate to the family at dinner. Then the pair flew off, and that was all—or so it seemed. I realize now that slight flash of living color was God's harbinger with a special message of hope for me.

Next day I received a letter from my old doctor friend, who had first diagnosed my difficulty. She wrote, "Perhaps the most important reaction I have to your problem is that you do seem to be responding to your own conflicts much as most people do. If when this reaches you, you feel calmer and are able to get some perspective, then you may know what you really want to do to improve the whole pattern. Any thoughtful person may have doubts about his own faith, and certainly about that of others, so your 'rebellion' about this is not foolish, only natural. Perhaps if you decide you've done your best, you can smile and be peaceful and be able to live with yourself. From my view, this is where we all start."

The question was, how did I set about "improving the whole pattern"? Painstakingly I tried to rebuild, to follow the wise advice, and to learn to live above my feelings. With no little trepidation I drew up the following ambitious outline:

1. Take all medication prescribed by the doctor, whether or not it seems to be helping.
2. Try to start, and if possible, to finish some extra household task each day that I don't want to do.
3. Improve body tone by exercising whether or not I want to get off the couch.
4. Answer some of the piled-up correspondence, positively and cheerfully, not seeking sympathy for my plight.
5. Go back to the Sunday School advice: "God first, others second, myself last."
6. Do *something* for the Lord, no matter how weak I feel spiritually and physically. (How often I had advised others to flex their spiritual muscles if they would avoid atrophy, to put their talent to work and not to bury it.)

7. Stifle hurt feelings and animosity at home, regardless of provocation; be as sweet to the family as to outsiders!

8. Resume daily devotions, praying for guidance and joy; exchanging feelings for facts, especially in the worry department. Know and practice replacing the stored depressions with the stored promises of Scripture in my subconscious mind.

9. Put myself in God's pathway, not chiding myself when attention wanders, but giving him the glory when it doesn't. Use my limited strength not selfishly, but for others.

The last rule was the hardest. I hadn't been able to endure myself, far less love myself, so how could I obey God's injunction? Obviously he wanted me to regard myself with respect.

The first step back toward Christian normality came when a neighbor was suddenly taken ill. I was able to help her in conversation and prayer.

Soon afterward I heard an unusual testimony from an outstanding artist. He was a Christian who had turned away from the Lord. One Sunday he stopped in a small church in France where he had sung the year before. An American serviceman was singing the same hymn he had once sung, and was doing it badly. The singer realized that God had taken a weak vessel and had blessed it to his use, that what counts in God's sight is not so much ability as availability. I prayed to make myself available and to have God's message on my lips and in my life.

Soon after that I was asked to speak to a church group. My old fluency had deserted me; how could I address them? I reviewed my personal "Bill of Rights." Yes, I must pay my "do's"! And the verse came: "I can do all things through Christ which strengtheneth me" (Philippians 4:13).

Perhaps you can see now why I have become an avid cardinal-watcher! I am absolutely convinced that God sent that little bit of red into my life to tell me that depression was not his plan for me. He had something better in mind, and he was going to bring it to pass. Odd, isn't it, how a tiny symbol like a cardinal can be used of God to capture the imagination and help to heal the hurts of past and present, and (since we are mortals) probably of future struggles.

Word of my fondness for cardinals seems to have filtered through to some of my friends, who have grasped the deeper significance of the name. One dear friend told me recently that the word *cardinal* comes from the Latin *cardo* which means "a hinge or turning point." Think of it! And the dictionary says there is a related Greek word which means "the waving branch of a tree"! Today the adjective *cardinal* appears to mean something of basic and pre-eminent importance. To which I can add, "and how!"

During the winter while I wait for spring to come, bringing my little feathered friend in person, I thank God for good furnace heat. I glance around with a smile at the perky cardinal plate on the wall in our front room, and the stained-glass cardinals flying toward each other in our family room windows.

I put on the teakettle, then heat the pot for delicious brew, British fashion, except that mine is about a third as strong. Then I pour the fragrant, steaming tea into my cardinal mug. Refreshed, I step to my small antique desk and prepare to visit with a friend on the West Coast via some cardinal notepaper.

I never tell my husband when I am better. I don't need to. He knows. Even our pets know. Today as I write, I realize it has been a long time since I was cruelly depressed. I sit quietly, collecting my thoughts, realizing that something has happened at last to the dreadful cycle of a few weeks "up" and a few weeks "down."

Yes, I still sag, but only briefly, mildly, and without suicidal desperation. I know that people are praying for me, and I murmur several times a day, "Thank you, Jesus." The vital processes slow down; my head doesn't seem to "work right"; but rather than feel sad, I just feel inefficient. For a few nights there is heavy slumber, and then, praise God, "the fairies come," Six weeks pass without a slump, and I know the hangman's noose has loosened. Life becomes a great, swelling doxology.

Last Christmas I was able to discover anew the truth of Paul's testimony to the power of the living Christ. An opportunity came to join a group that was visiting hospitals. At the time I was feeling weak, but my husband said, "I think you'll feel worse if you don't go." So I went back to the familiar haunts, and found it a victorious experience. As I gave of myself I was blessed in return.

Recently in Catherine Marshall's book *Beyond Our Selves* I reread the chapter "The Prayer of Relinquishment," and discovered afresh the difference between resignation, which is negative, and acceptance, which is positive. I altered my attitude toward my own condition, applying the principle set forth by the author: "Acceptance leaves the door of hope wide open to God's creative plan." I began—oh, so timidly—to thank God for the illness that was bringing me closer to him.

It has been several years since I grappled with myself before the medicine cabinet. Our two sons have grown up and gone, but with maturity has come understanding and love. A car door opens and shuts—my husband is home early from the office. As I stop to give my hair a final pat and add a trace of his favorite cologne, I note that my face is wearing a carefree expression in what I had once thought of as "the dark mirror." Am I "high"? Am I "low"? I know I am not out of the woods by a long way. But I go to the door with a smile of expectancy on my lips, arms outstretched to embrace him. Over his shoulder I see high in the oak tree a cardinal's nest, and I think, "Thank you, Lord, for the blessing of hope."